SNAKES BOOK

Everything You Need To Know
About Reptile Snakes

SMAUEL FERDINARD

Setting out on a quest to comprehend the complex world of snakes not only reveals the fascinating features of these reptiles but also serves a vital purpose in debunking myths that frequently envelop them in mystery.

Snakes have long captivated people due to their wide range of traits, unusual adaptations, and important ecological responsibilities.

People who explore the world of these mysterious animals come away with a greater understanding of biodiversity and the significance of coexisting with the natural world.

1. Why Learn About Snakes? Learning about snakes is like discovering the mysteries of a long-lived and hardy ancestry that has flourished for millions of years in a variety of environments. Despite their sometimes-misconstrued image, snakes are essential to ecosystems because they help control pests, preserve ecological balance, and act as environmental health indicators.

Understanding snakes helps us to appreciate their evolutionary adaptations, such as their interesting movement patterns and deadly fangs, as well as their crucial role in preserving the delicate balance of nature. Furthermore, learning about snakes helps us live in harmony with the environment by improving our capacity to live safely beside these animals.

2. Common Myths: Fear and confusion have been sustained throughout history by persistent myths about snakes. To promote a more knowledgeable and courteous attitude toward these amazing reptiles, these myths must be cleared up.

Contrary to popular assumption, most snakes are not poisonous, and many are vital for maintaining pest populations under control.

By exposing falsehoods about snakes, we may reduce unjustified fear and emphasize the significance of protecting these amazing animals. People may support the conservation of snake species and advance a more accurate knowledge of their role in the complex web of life by challenging and correcting misunderstandings.

Exploring the world of snakes provides a singular chance to recognize the wonders of biodiversity, solve the riddles of a long-standing ancestry, and dispel myths about these amazing animals.

We can foster a sense of cohabitation and help to preserve these vital elements of our natural world through knowledge and understanding.

CHAPTER ONE
Snake Basics

3. What Are Snakes?

Snakes are amazing animals that have piqued people's interest for ages and are members of the Serpentes suborder. These limbless reptiles, which descended from predecessors with legs, have demonstrated extraordinary adaptability in their survival strategies by adapting to a wide variety of habitats.

With more than 3,000 species currently known to exist, snakes can be found almost anywhere in the world, including frigid tundras, deserts, and thick rainforests. Although they differ from one another, all snakes have traits in common that set them apart from other reptiles, which makes them a special and fascinating group in the animal realm.

4. Variety between Snake Species

The diversity of colors, patterns, and sizes found in the world of snakes is astounding.

The variety of snake species is astounding, ranging from the tiny thread snake, which is just a few inches long, to the enormous reticulated python, which may grow to be over 20 feet long.

Because snakes can adapt to a wide range of ecological niches, specialized species have emerged. Examples of these are arboreal snakes, which live in trees, burrowing species, which explore underground spaces, and aquatic serpents, which are perfectly suited to live in water.

They also have quite different diets; some are staunch carnivores, while others have a wider range of eating preferences. Examining the wide variety of snake species offers insight into the complex network of habitats they live in, demonstrating the flexibility and tenacity of these amazing animals.

5. Anatomy of the Serpent

The intricate anatomy of snakes, which has changed over millions of years to fit their particular lifestyle, must be studied to comprehend them completely.

One distinguishing characteristic is the lack of limbs, which is made up of an extended torso and unique scales that help with protection and movement. Another amazing feature of snake jaw construction is that several species can dislocate their lower jaw, which enables them to eat prey that is much larger than their heads.

Snakes are adept predators because of their sensory organs, which include forked tongues that aid in smell detection and, in some species, specialized pits for infrared vision.

An interior examination reveals complex reproductive organs that differ between snake species and effective digestive systems designed for the ingestion of complete prey. Comprehending the anatomy of snakes is essential for comprehending not only their evolutionary history but also their behaviors, ecological functions in their particular habitats, and survival tactics.

CHAPTER TWO
Snake Behavior

6. Snake Senses

Snakes have an amazing variety of senses that enable them to live and navigate their surroundings despite not having standard ears. Their jawbones, which connect to their inner ears, are their main means of perceiving sound and vibrations. They can hear ground vibrations thanks to this special adaption, which helps them identify potential threats or approaching prey. Furthermore, snakes have an acute sense of smell, which is enhanced by the Jacobson's organ on the roof of their mouths. With the help of this unique organ, they can identify and interpret chemical clues in the atmosphere, which helps them find prey and possible partners.

In addition, snakes have very developed eyes, albeit different species have different levels of vision.

While some snakes rely more on their other senses, some have exceptional vision and can see well in dim light. With all of these sensory adaptations, snakes have an extensive toolkit for perceiving their environment, which helps them to move around and engage with it.

6. Snake Movement

Snake mobility is an amazing feat of efficiency and adaptability. Snakes have no appendages, but they are incredibly agile and can move through a wide range of terrain. The most typical way for a snake to move is through lateral undulation, in which it presses its body against objects to create a sequence of curves that help it move forward. Another technique is sidewinding, in which the snake rolls its body laterally and is very helpful in sandy settings. Arboreal snakes can move in a concertina manner, grasping objects with certain portions of their bodies and extending others forward.

Comprehending the aforementioned movement patterns is vital to comprehending the ecological niche and survival tactics of snakes.

It also clarifies how they may hunt, avoid predators, and adjust to a variety of environments.

8. Feeding Patterns

The various feeding habits exhibited by snakes are determined by their species, size, and habitat. Some are opportunistic feeders, taking whatever is available, while others are specialist hunters with a taste for certain species. Because of their extremely flexible jaws and capacity to unhinge their lower jaw, which enables them to swallow prey larger than their heads, snakes mainly swallow their prey whole.

Constrictor snakes use constriction to suffocate their victims, while venomous snakes use their poison to kill or immobilize their prey before consuming it. The frequency of feeding varies; depending on the species, size, and availability of prey, some snakes may go weeks or even months without eating.

Comprehending the dietary patterns of reptiles is essential for handling them in captivity and offers a valuable understanding of the intricate equilibrium between predators and prey in their native environments.

9. The Life Cycle and Reproduction

Snakes have a wide variety of reproductive techniques, just like their species. The majority of snake species are sexually reproducing, and some even have complex courtship rituals. There are two types of fertilization: internal and external. While some snakes lay eggs, others give birth to live offspring. The length of the incubation period and the quantity of progeny differ greatly between species.

Since most snake species do not show parental care, young snakes are frequently left on their own after they are born or hatch. Their early independence is essential to their survival since they have to pick up hunting and predator avoidance skills fast.

Comprehending the complexities of snake reproduction and its different life stages is essential for conservation endeavors and can provide valuable perspectives on the function of snakes in preserving the equilibrium of ecosystems. It also offers vital information to anybody involved in managing and raising these amazing reptiles in captivity.

CHAPTER THREE
Snake Habitats

10. Where Snakes Live

Snakes are extraordinarily versatile animals that can live happily in a wide range of environmental conditions all over the world. Snakes have successfully inhabited almost every region on Earth, from arid landscapes to lush rainforests and from scorching deserts to freshwater environments. Gaining knowledge of their favored habitats is essential to comprehend their behavior, breeding, and general survival tactics.

For example, the forest floor of tropical rainforests is home to an amazing diversity of snake species. These snakes frequently hide in vegetation and leaf litter, taking advantage of the thick growth for cover and ambush hunting. In the meantime, snakes in arid deserts have adapted to survive extremely hot weather by hiding out in the sand during the day and coming out at night to hunt.

Numerous snake species can be found in aquatic settings. Some people are skilled swimmers who can easily navigate lakes, rivers, and coastal seas. These snakes' water lifestyle is made easier by their streamlined bodies and unique scales.

Others, such as sea snakes, have developed to only exist in saltwater habitats; they have modified lungs to enable them to take in oxygen from the surrounding air.

11. Snake Environment Adaptations

Snakes have developed a wide range of adaptations that enable them to flourish in their particular environments. Their behaviors, physical traits, and hunting techniques all reflect these adaptations. For example, snakes that live in desert regions frequently have scales that reflect sunlight, which lowers heat absorption. Those in colder climates, on the other hand, might have darker scales that are more heat-absorbing.

Residing in diverse environments across the globe, venomous snakes have evolved strong venoms to control prey and protect themselves from apex predators. Certain animals can sense heat from their pits and identify warm-blooded prey even in the darkness. Because of their prehensile tails for grasping branches and their slender bodies for effortless movement through vegetation, arboreal snakes are adapted to live in trees.

Comprehending these adaptations highlights the delicate balance between snake biology and the habitats they live in, while also illuminating the wonderful diversity of snakes.

12. Conservation and Endangering

Threats to the survival of many snake species exist, despite their amazing adaptability.

Many human actions, including pollution, habitat degradation, and climate change, are contributing factors to the global fall in snake populations. Furthermore, misinformation and fear frequently cause snakes to be persecuted, which results in intentional murders.

For ecosystems to remain in their delicate balance and for biodiversity to persist, conservation activities are essential. Conservation methods must include measures to preserve snake habitats, control the pet trade, and inform the public about the value of snakes in ecosystems. Programs for captive breeding contribute to the protection of endangered species by offering a possible means of reintroducing them into the wild.

To solve the issues that snakes face, a comprehensive strategy including local communities, scientists, and policymakers is ultimately required. By acknowledging the significance of these mysterious animals in preserving ecological balance, we can endeavor to guarantee a sustainable coexistence of snakes and the habitats they inhabit.

CHAPTER FOUR
Snake Identification

13.　　Identifying Venomous vs. Non-venomous Snakes:

Revealing the Hidden Armour of the Serpent

Not only is it important to identify the species of snake, but it's also critical to differentiate between venomous and non-venomous snakes.

It may be the difference between life and death to grasp the salient features that set the two apart.

We shall explore the intriguing realm of snake venom, fangs, and defensive mechanisms in this part. Acquire the ability to interpret the cues that suggest whether a snake is something to be enjoyed from a safe distance or should be handled carefully.

14. Identifying Common Snake Species: A Color and Pattern Palette

Snakes display a remarkable range of patterns, colors, and behaviors. This section will act as a field guide to help you recognize some of the most prevalent species of snakes. We will examine the distinctive characteristics that set each species apart, from the breathtaking diamondback pattern of a rattlesnake to the sophisticated markings of a corn snake. This will provide you the ability to recognize these sly neighbors whether you come across them in the wild or your backyard.

15. How to Navigate the Serpent Safari with a Field Guide to Snakes

Get yourself a thorough field guide to snakes; it's a need for every aspiring naturalist or herpetologist. You can find a useful how-to instruction for using field guides in this section. We'll go over the essential characteristics to consider while identifying snakes, such as preferred habitats, head forms, and scale patterns. We'll also discuss how crucial it is to comprehend a snake's behavior to make an accurate identification. This field guide is an important tool for anyone interested in learning more about these interesting reptiles, regardless of experience level.

• Section 15.1: Texture and Scale Patterns: Deciphering the Signature of the Serpent

Section 15.2: An Insight into the Serpent's Soul through Head Shapes and Jaw Structures

• Section 15.3: Preferences for Habitats: Locating the Slithering Inhabitants

By the time this chapter ends, you should be able to confidently identify common snake species in a variety of situations in addition to being able to tell venomous from non-venomous snakes.

Equipped with your field guide, you'll go out on a quest to explore the complex realm of snake identification, developing a greater understanding of these fascinating animals.

CHAPTER FIVE
<u>Interacting With Snakes</u>

16. Safety Precautions

Safety must always come first when handling snakes as pets or while traveling through regions where snake activity is known. The following are important safety measures to think about:

1. Wear Appropriate Clothes: Wear long pants, boots, and gloves while in locations where snakes are a risk. In the event of unintentional contact, this can offer an extra degree of security.

A. When engaging in outdoor activities in areas where snakes are present, it is advisable to wear snake gaiters. These are protective coverings that encircle your lower legs and ankles, providing an additional layer of defense against potential bites.

an. Remain on Designated trails: When hiking or exploring natural reserves, stay on well-traveled trails. Steer clear of underbrush and dense grass where snakes can be hiding.

Day. Be Wary When Lifting Rocks and Logs: Be wary of lifting rocks or logs because they can be hiding places for snakes. From a safe distance, use a stick or other instrument to gently lift possible hiding places.

e. When in places where snakes are common, always have a snake bite kit with you. To lessen the effects of venom, these kits usually contain supplies like bandages, antiseptic wipes, and a suction device.

g. Know the Local Snakes: Become knowledgeable about the local species of snakes. Variations in the behaviors and venom kinds of snakes can impact the appropriate response in the event of a confrontation.

17. Snake Contact

It can be frightening to come upon a snake in the wild or by accident in your surroundings. Here's how to proceed:

1. Remain Calm: Remain silent and composed. Many snakes will not bite unless they perceive a threat. Anxiety can make things worse.

A. Back Off Gradually: Gradually retreat from the snake to give it room. Steer clear of abrupt movements since these could agitate the snake.

an. Identify the Snake: Attempt to identify the snake from a distance if it is safe to do so. In the event of a bite, this information may be helpful to medical experts.

Day. Do Not Touch: Unless you are a qualified professional, never try to handle a wild snake. Even harmless snakes may bite if they sense danger.

e. Notify Others: To avoid unintentional contact, alert others about the snake if you're in a public location.

g. Report Sightings: Notify the appropriate wildlife organizations or the local authorities of any sightings of snakes. This information enhances public safety by tracking snake populations.

18. Taking Care of Snakes (If Required)

It may occasionally be required to handle a snake, particularly for researchers, professionals, and pet owners. Observe these rules:

1. Employ the Right Equipment: If handling is necessary, keep a safe distance between you and the snake by using the right tools, such as snake tongs or hooks.

A. Approach gently and carefully: To prevent frightening the snake, approach it gently and carefully. A defensive reaction could be elicited by sudden movements.

an. Support the Snake's Body: To prevent putting too much pressure or stress on a snake's spine when lifting it, offer support along its entire length.

Day. Wash Your Hands Completely: Make sure to wash your hands completely after handling a snake. To stop the possible spread of bacteria or parasites, this is crucial.

e. Understand Local Laws: Recognize and abide by local laws about the care and keeping of snakes in captivity. Certain operations may require permissions due to the protection of certain species.

You can reduce hazards and encourage a safer relationship with these intriguing but potentially hazardous animals by adhering to these safety precautions and handling rules for snakes.

CHAPTER SIX
Snake Myths And Legends

19. Snakes in Culture and Mythology

Snakes have been integral parts of many nations' mythologies and cultures throughout history. These mysterious animals, which represent a variety of symbolic meanings and mythological stories, have been both adored and dreaded.

19.1 Egypt in Ancient Times: The Sign of Rebirth

The snake, especially the cobra, played a major role in ancient Egyptian mythology. Pharaohs' crowns were ornamented with the uraeus, a symbol of divine authority and protection. The idea of rejuvenation and rebirth was symbolized by a snake's skin shedding, which was consistent with Egyptian beliefs of the afterlife.

19.2 Snakes as Guardians in Hinduism

Serpents are important in Hindu mythology and are frequently connected to gods like Shiva and Vishnu.

The snake, also known as the naga, is associated with fertility and protection. The Hindu mythology surrounding Ananta Shesha, the thousand-headed serpent on which Vishnu rests, serves as an example of the cosmic significance snakes are given.

19.3 Chinese Mythology: The Relationship with Dragons

In Chinese mythology, dragons and serpents are frequently combined, with dragons being viewed as strong, kind animals. Dragons and snakes are similar concepts that represent longevity, wisdom, and imperial might. The Snake is one of the twelve animals in the Chinese zodiac, which highlights its cultural significance.

19.4 Wisdom Serpent in Greek Mythology

Snakes were connected to knowledge and healing in ancient Greece.

Asclepius, the deity of healing, is associated with the rod of Asclepius, a staff wrapped with a snake that represents medicine. The story of the goddess

Medusa, whose hair turned into serpents, symbolizes the dual nature of snakes as both dangerous and kind.

19.5 Native American Customs: The Meaning of Metamorphosis

Many American Indian tribes have symbols related to snakes in their mythology.

Many people interpret the snake's skin shedding as a metaphor for their rebirth and metamorphosis.

For example, the Horned Serpent, a formidable creature connected to thunder and rain, is highly revered by the Cherokee people.

19.6 Symbolism in the Bible: The Snake in Eden

The serpent is portrayed in the Bible, especially in the book of Genesis, as a crafty and dishonest being that seduces Adam and Eve in the Garden of Eden. This story has shaped how snakes are perceived in the West as representations of evil and temptation.

20. Common Myths About Snakes

Snakes are fascinating creatures that are often misunderstood, leading to different myths that contribute to fear and unfavorable attitudes toward them, despite their ecological significance and rich cultural heritage.

20.1 Every Snake Is Poisonous

One widespread myth is that all snakes are dangerous to people and contain venom.

The vast majority of snake species are not poisonous and serve vital functions in managing rodent populations.

20.2 Snakes Seek Humans and Are Aggressive

Contrary to popular assumption, snakes are typically shy and would rather stay away from people. Rather than the snake actively seeking out confrontation, most snake bites happen when humans accidentally step on or disturb them.

20.3 The Myth of the "Triangle Head"

There is a common misperception that snakes with rounded heads are not venomous, but those with triangular heads are. Many non-poisonous snakes also have triangular heads, while only a small number of venomous snakes do.

20.4 Snakes Pursue People

It's a fallacy that snakes aggressively seek out humans. Snakes' natural tendency is to flee, but they may come closer if they sense danger. When a snake feels surrounded, it often tries to find cover or flee, which is how it perceives being pursued.

20.5 Milk-Drinking Snakes

It's a common misperception that snakes are drawn to milk. Although they may be inquisitive and investigate different smells, snakes are not attracted to milk. This belief has given rise to hazardous customs that may be harmful to snakes' health, such as feeding them milk.

It is imperative to comprehend the diverse array of myths surrounding snakes and eliminate widespread misunderstandings to promote a more knowledgeable and peaceful coexistence with these amazing animals.

CHAPTER SEVEN
Keeping Snakes As Pets

21. Uncovering the Serpentine Realm in the World of Pet Snakes

Introducing the intriguing world of pet snakes, where slithering friends add a certain touch to the exotic pet category. There is an incredible variety of snake species available for captivity, ranging from the sleek and stealthy to the brightly patterned. This chapter will examine the nuances of caring for these fascinating pets, including the many kinds, their lifestyles, and the pleasures they provide to snake lovers around the globe.

22. Selecting the Appropriate Snake: A Cobra for Every Guardian

One of the most important steps in guaranteeing a satisfying experience with pet ownership is choosing the ideal snake for your interests and lifestyle. It is crucial to comprehend the various requirements and personalities of various snake species, regardless of your level of familiarity with reptiles. This section will walk you through the process of selecting the ideal snake for you, taking into account characteristics like size, temperament, and particular care needs.

Snakes range in size from gentle ball pythons to the more daring corn snakes.

• Beginner-Friendly Snakes: Some species, such as ball pythons, corn snakes, and garter snakes, are well-known for their gentle disposition and comparatively simple maintenance needs, making them ideal for novice snake keepers.

We'll look at the qualities that make these snakes the best for novices and share information about their nutrition and habitat requirements.

• Intermediate and Advanced Options: As your knowledge increases, you may find yourself drawn to more difficult species such as arboreal snakes, pythons, and boas. To assist you in making an informed choice based on your degree of experience and commitment, this section will describe the special concerns and obligations associated with these snakes.

• Specialized Environments: The optimal habitats for various snake species vary. We will go over the particular needs for each, whether you're interested in a semi-aquatic enclosure, an arboreal habitat, or a terrestrial setting, to make sure your snake is safe and happy in its new home.

24. Taking Care of Your Serpentine Companion: A Guide to Snake Husbandry

A pet snake's health and well-being greatly depend on proper care and husbandry. This section will offer a thorough how-to instructions for setting up the ideal habitat for your snake, including important subjects like:

• Enclosure Setup: describing the nuances of setting up a safe and cozy enclosure, such as substrate selections, humidity levels, temperature gradients, and the value of hiding places.

• Nutrition and Feeding: Examining the dietary requirements for pet snakes, including selecting suitable prey and planning a feeding regimen.

We will cover typical questions about feeding frequency, prey size, and possible nutritional health problems.

• Handling and Interaction: Providing tips on how to deal with snakes tactfully, establish rapport, and read their body language. We'll go over the dos and don'ts of interaction to make sure you and your snake have a happy, stress-free relationship.

• Health Monitoring: Acknowledging typical health problems and identifying indicators of a healthy snake. To keep your snake healthy, we'll offer advice on routine health examinations, veterinarian care, and preventative measures.

• Reproduction and Breeding: This section will cover the fundamentals of snake reproduction, breeding considerations, and the duties involved in caring for snake progeny for individuals who wish to advance their snake-keeping endeavors.

CHAPTER EIGHT
Snake Conservation

24. The Importance of Snake Conservation

Snakes are creatures that are frequently misunderstood and despised, but they are essential to preserving the delicate balance of ecosystems worldwide. Because they are essential components of many food chains, they help keep rodent populations under control, which helps stop agricultural loss and disease transmission. Additionally, by controlling the populations of small animals, birds, and amphibians, snakes play a critical role in preserving biodiversity.

The goal of snake conservation is to preserve not just individual species but also the complex web of relationships that snakes have within their respective habitats. As predators, they keep prey populations healthy and stop some species from proliferating unrestrained, which may upset entire ecosystems.

 In addition, snakes themselves contribute to the general biodiversity of their ecosystems by acting as prey for larger predators.

In addition to their ecological importance, snakes are quite helpful in medical studies.

Certain snake species' venom contains substances that have been researched for possible medical uses, such as the creation of analgesics and anticoagulants. Maintaining snake populations guarantees that these biological resources will be available for use in future scientific research.

However, several factors, such as habitat loss, climate change, illegal trafficking, and persecution due to false beliefs and fears, pose a threat to snake populations. To lessen these dangers and guarantee the survival of these amazing animals, conservation initiatives are crucial.

25. Preserving Snake Environments

Protecting the habitats of snakes is one of the main goals of snake conservation.

Like many other species, snakes rely heavily on particular environments to survive.

Their numbers are seriously at risk from the destruction and modification of natural habitats. The following are important tactics for preserving snake habitats:

1. Preservation of Habitat: To ensure that snake habitats are conserved, it is essential to create protected places like national parks and wildlife reserves. These places offer a haven where snakes can survive, procreate, and engage in their normal activities without worrying about their habitat being destroyed right away.

A. Habitat Restoration: Restoring adequate habitats for snakes can be done in situations where their habitats have been damaged.

This could entail handling pollution problems, managing water supplies, and replanting native plants.

an. Creation of Wildlife Corridors: To connect disparate habitats, wildlife corridors must be established.

Snakes can travel between different areas through these corridors in search of food, partners, and good places to breed. This is especially crucial for species whose home ranges are large.

Day. Community Involvement: It is essential to include nearby communities in efforts to save habitat. The long-term success of conservation programs is ensured by educating communities about the value of snakes in preserving ecological balance and integrating them into sustainable resource management methods.

e. Taking Care of Climate Change: Snake habitats are seriously threatened by climate change.

The long-term sustainability of snake populations depends on putting climate change mitigation measures into action, such as cutting greenhouse gas emissions and modifying conservation plans to account for shifting climatic circumstances.

g. Legislation and Regulation: It's imperative to put legislation protecting snake habitats into effect and enforce them. This includes controlling land use, stopping unauthorized development and logging, and making sure that operations in environmentally sensitive areas are carried out in an environmentally responsible manner.

Conservationists can significantly increase the chances of ensuring the survival of these intriguing and critically essential reptiles by concentrating on the preservation and restoration of snake habitats. Effective snake habitat conservation requires a trifecta of scientific research, community involvement, and legislative initiatives.

CHAPTER NINE
Resources For Snake Enthusiasts

26. Recommended Books and Websites

Explore the fascinating world of snakes with a carefully chosen list of websites and books that are suitable for beginners as well as experts.

These websites address a wide range of subjects, including behavior, ecology, and conservation in addition to snake identification.

Novels:

• Chris Mattison's "The Complete Guide to Snakes of North America" is an extensive reference book with beautiful photos and in-depth details on the many kinds of snakes that can be found throughout the continent.

• Harry W. Greene's "Snakes: The Evolution of Mystery in Nature" delves into the evolutionary background and engrossing tales of snakes, masterfully penned by the well-known herpetologist.

• Roger Conant and Joseph T. Collins' "A Field Guide to Reptiles and Amphibians: Eastern and Central North America" is a priceless tool for recognizing a broad variety of reptiles, including snakes, throughout Eastern and Central North America, however, it is not just limited to snakes.

• "Venomous Snakes of the World" by Mark O'Shea: This book offers comprehensive information on the world's venomous snakes, their biology, and the significance of venom in their ecosystem, making it a great read for anybody interested in venomous animals.

webpages

• The Center for Snake Conservation: Dedicated to protecting snake species, this group offers insightful data on the biology, ecology, and conservation initiatives of snakes.

• Field Herp Forum: Connect with other herpetology enthusiasts and post pictures and anecdotes of your snake encounters.

This forum is a great place to get knowledge from the experiences of others.

• The Reptile Database: a thorough database with taxonomy, distribution maps, and references for reptile species, including snakes.

• I Naturalist: Take part in citizen science by adding your observations of snakes to an international database. Through community contributions, this platform also aids in the identification of species.

26. Herpetological Associations

Engage with respectable organizations devoted to the research and preservation of amphibians and reptiles to make connections with other snake enthusiasts and advance the subject of herpetology.

Establishments:

• The Herpetologists' League: An international organization that supports herpetology-related scientific research, instruction, and conservation.

• The Orianne Society: Dedicated to the preservation of amphibians and reptiles, this group carries out studies and carries out conservation campaigns to save various snake species and their natural environments.

• International Herpetological conference: Join the yearly conference to network with professionals, scholars, and herpetology enthusiasts.

• Snakebite Healing and Education Society: Committed to promoting knowledge about first aid, medical treatment for snakebites, and avoidance of snakebite injuries.

29. Snake-related Activities and Events

Take part in events and activities that are geared for snake aficionados of all skill levels to fully immerse yourself in the world of snakes.

There is something for everyone, regardless of your interests in educational programs, field trips, or environmental efforts.

Activities and Events:

• Snake Awareness and Handling Workshops: Attend workshops organized by nearby wildlife organizations or herpetological societies to gain knowledge on the identification, behavior, and safe handling of snakes.

• Reptile Expos and Shows: Visit reptile expos to get up close and personal with a range of snake species, network with breeders and dealers, and learn about safe reptile management.

• Guided Herping Tours: Take part in field visits that are conducted by knowledgeable herpetologists to discover natural habitats, see snakes in the wild, and discover the ecology of these animals.

• Volunteer programs for snake conservation: Assist with conservation efforts by volunteering for organizations that conduct research on snakes and restore their habitat.

Through the use of these tools, networking with like-minded people, and participation in snake-related events, you can contribute to the conservation and responsible ownership of these amazing reptiles while also learning more about and developing respect for them.

Conclusion

We've discovered a plethora of marvels that make snakes genuinely fascinating animals after exploring the fascinating world of reptiles.

 The world of snakes is a tribute to the complexity of nature, from their many species and distinctive adaptations to their vital ecological roles.

We've looked at their fascinating habits, complex poisonous systems, and diverse methods of environment navigation.

Beyond the biological, however, our research has also shown the diverse cultural value that snakes have throughout various communities.

These animals, which may be found in mythology, religion, and folklore throughout the world, have become profoundly ingrained in the human psyche as symbols of change, healing, or even dread.

As we get to the end of our investigation, it is critical to acknowledge the significance of conservation efforts for these mysterious creatures. Snakes suffer many issues that require our attention, including habitat loss, climate change, and misinformation. We can build a cohabitation that guarantees these species' longevity and the balance of ecosystems they contribute to by encouraging a greater awareness and respect for them.

Let us, in closing, continue to be in awe of and respectful of the amazing world of snakes. There's enough to learn and appreciate about these slithering marvels, regardless of your level of interest or trepidation.

May this exploration serve as a reminder of the beauty and significance of every creature, no matter how misinterpreted or misrepresented, as we negotiate the intricate web of coexistence with the numerous species in our world.